Notes

Summary

Summary

Summary

Notes

Summary

Summary

Summary

Summary

Summary

Summary

Notes

Summary

Summary

Notes

Summary

Summary

Notes

Summary

Summary

Notes

Summary

Summary

Notes

Summary

Summary

Notes

Summary

Summary

Notes

Summary

Summary

Summary

Notes

Summary

Summary

Summary

Summary

Notes

Summary

Notes

Summary

Summary

Notes

Summary

Summary

Notes

Summary

Summary

Notes

Summary

Notes

Summary

Notes

Summary

Summary

Notes

Summary

Summary

Summary

Notes

Summary

Summary

Notes

Summary

Summary

Notes

Summary

Summary

Notes

Summary

Summary

Notes

Summary

Notes

Summary

Summary

Summary

Notes

Summary

Summary

Notes

Summary

Notes

Summary

Notes

Summary

Notes

Summary

Notes

Summary

Summary

Notes

Summary

Summary

Notes

Summary

Summary

Summary

Notes

Summary

Summary

Notes

Summary

Summary

Notes

Summary

Summary

Notes

Summary

Notes

Summary

Notes

Summary

Summary

Summary

Summary

Notes

Summary

Summary

Notes

Summary

Summary

Notes

Summary

Summary

Summary

Notes

Summary

Summary

Notes

Summary

Summary

Summary

Summary

Summary

Notes

Summary

Notes

Summary

Summary

Notes

Summary

Summary

Notes

Summary

Summary

Notes

Summary

Summary

Notes

Summary

Summary

Notes

Summary

Made in the USA
Middletown, DE
24 July 2018